Our Pets

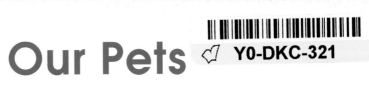

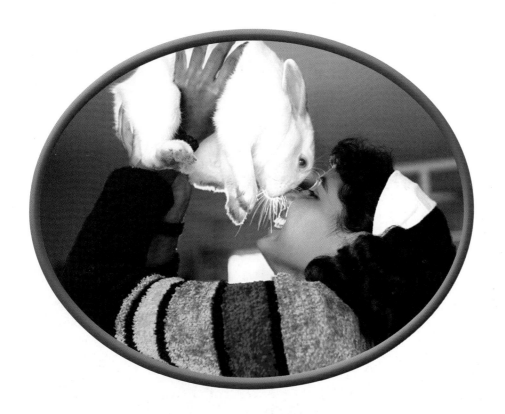

by Gregory Michaels

A dog is a pet.
I like my dog.

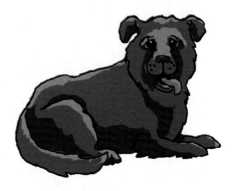

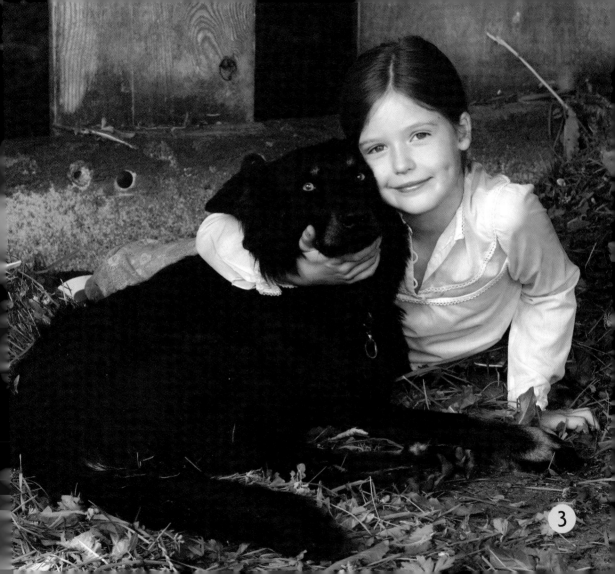

A fish is a pet.
I like my fish.

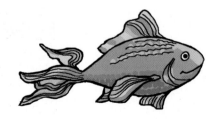

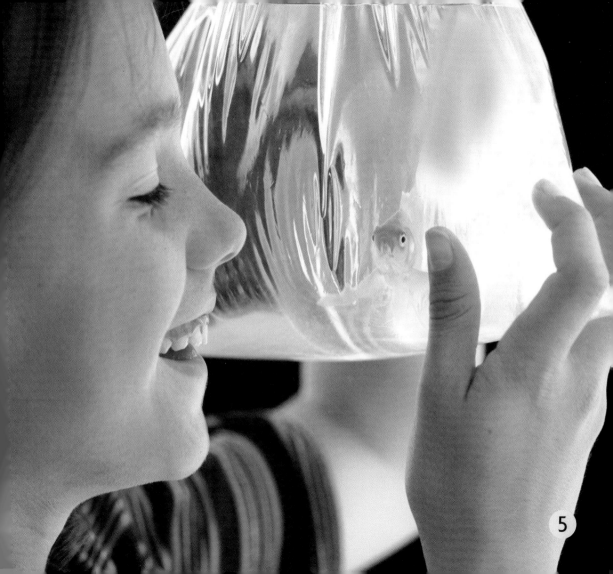

A bird is a pet.
I like my bird.

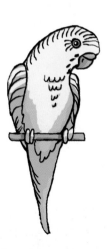

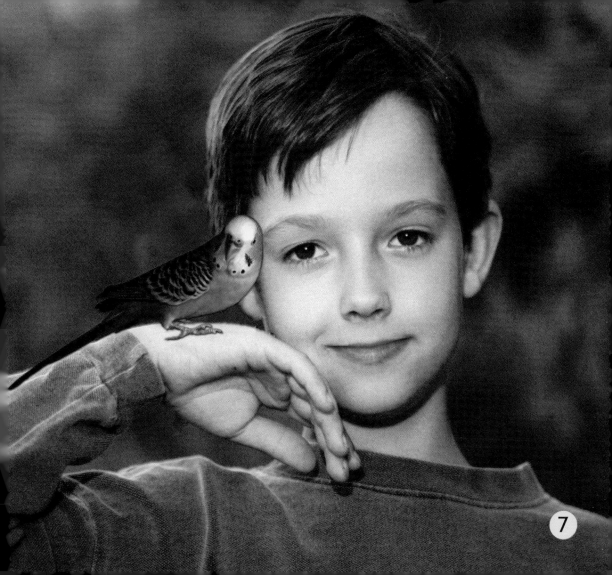

A pony is a pet.
I like my pony.

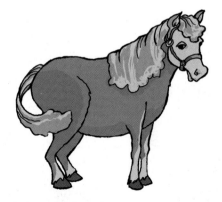

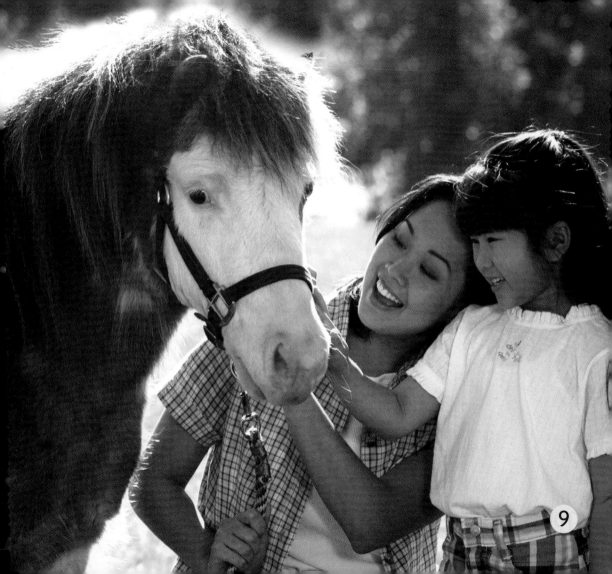

A cat is a pet.
I like my cat.

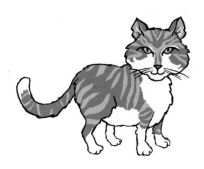

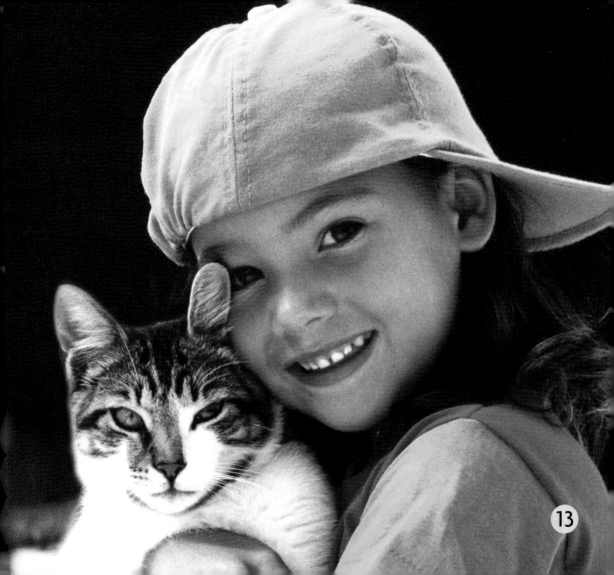

I like my pet.

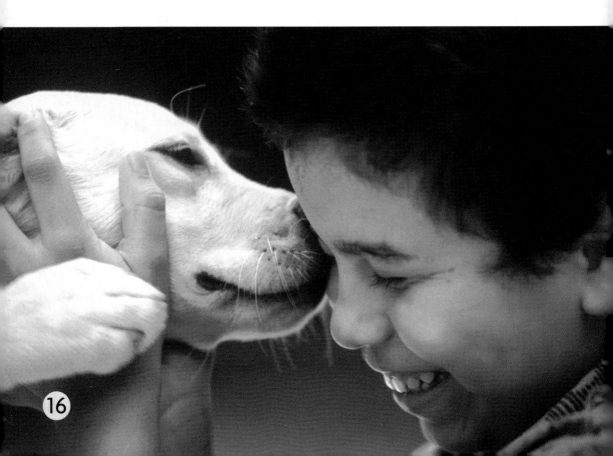